The MVPs of Education

Strategies for Combating the Teacher Shortage and Diversifying the Teacher Workforce

Blake Nathan

THE
WRITER'S
GAME

The Writers Game

The MVPs of Education

Strategies for Combating the Teacher
Shortage and Diversifying the Teacher
Workforce

Blake Nathan

THE
WRITER'S
GAME

The Writers Game

Book Cover by The Writers Game

Illustrations by The Writers Game

First Edition | 2023

The Writers Game

8936 Northpointe Executive Park Drive, Ste 260,

Huntersville, NC 28078

BLAKE NATHAN

info@thewritersgame.com

www.thewritersgame.com

ISBN: 979-8-9885156-6-1

eBook ISBN: 979-8-9885156-7-8

Printed in The United States of America

Contents

"Education is not preparation for life; education is life itself."

- John Dewey

To all the passionate educational leaders who strive to create a more inclusive and diverse learning environment,

This book, The MVPs of Education, is dedicated to you. Your unwavering commitment to shaping the future of education by diversifying the educational workforce is truly inspiring. You are the catalysts of change, understanding the profound impact that a diverse group of educators can have on the lives of students. With dedication and perseverance, you pave the way for equity, inclusivity, and cultural understanding within our schools.

May this book serve as a guiding light, providing you with strategies and insights to empower you in your mission. May it ignite your creativity, spark meaningful conversations, and offer practical solutions to build a vibrant and representative educational workforce.

Your efforts to cultivate a diverse community of educators not only enhance the educational experience but also empower students to embrace their own unique identities and thrive in an ever-changing world.

Thank you for your relentless pursuit of educational excellence and for creating spaces where every student feels seen, valued, and supported. Your leadership is transforming lives and shaping the future, one student at a time.

With deepest appreciation,

Blake Nathan

Educate Me

"Education is not the filling of a pail, but the lighting of a fire." - W.B. Yeats

Welcome to a journey that transcends the boundaries of traditional education. This book, titled "The MVPs of Education," is more than just a compilation of ideas; it's a passionate exploration of the transformative potential that lies within the diversification of our teaching workforce. As an organization dedicated to educational progress, we have come to a profound realization: we cannot navigate this path alone. We stand alongside a constellation of change-makers, each contributing their unique brilliance to the pursuit of a truly inclusive educational landscape.

For decades, the impact of desegregation, starting with the landmark Brown versus Board of Education case, has reverberated through our classrooms. The need for diversity among our teachers has become increasingly apparent, particularly within the black and brown communities. While we, as a small but mighty nonprofit organization, have accomplished remarkable feats, we are humbled by the presence of other remarkable players who are spearheading diversity efforts in different cities, states, and regions.

This book, born out of a deep-rooted belief in collaboration, aims to celebrate and magnify the achievements of these organizations. We want to show the education sector as a vibrant tapestry woven with the threads of countless initiatives, all working towards the same goal: recruiting and retaining more black and brown educators. By shining a spotlight on these remarkable institutions, we hope to inspire and empower others to follow suit.

Within the pages of this book, you will find a treasure trove of knowledge and inspiration. We present to you a comprehensive collection of best practices, innovative approaches, and success stories. As we share our thoughts and ideas, we invite you to join us in this movement of transformation. Let's explore the impact of Teacher Cadet Programs, collegiate initiatives, and professional development pathways—all tried and tested strategies already making a difference in the field.

One of the challenges we face is the lack of a centralized database or Rolodex of organizations dedicated to teacher diversification. While the White House has taken steps toward recruiting and retaining black and brown teachers, there is still a need to acknowledge and uplift grassroots organizations that are creating lasting change within their communities. These unsung heroes deserve recognition, and their stories deserve to be heard.

"The MVPs of Education" extends its reach beyond the confines of traditional education. It provides a compass, guiding school districts, charter school networks, private schools, and collegiate universities with education programs toward a more diverse and inclusive future. Superintendents seeking innovative strategies, city officials endeavoring to create impactful citywide initiatives, and state officials who aspire to attract diverse talent—all will find invaluable insights within these pages.

Drawing inspiration from the innovative thinking of leaders across the country, we explore groundbreaking ideas that transcend the boundaries of convention. Imagine a state where teachers are rewarded with no state income tax, as proposed by a forward-thinking candidate running for governor in Indiana. Such audacious ideas have the potential to revolutionize the teaching profession, empowering educators to keep more of their hard-earned money and channel it back into their classrooms.

This book addresses not only the teacher shortage crisis but also the imperative to nurture the economic upward mobility of our youth. In an era where the minority is now the majority, we face the challenge of preparing a skilled talent pool that can contribute to the growth and prosperity of our nation. By diversifying our teacher workforce, we unleash a ripple effect that stimulates economic progress, transforms communities, and propels the United States to the forefront of global leadership.

"The MVPs of Education" is a labor of love, driven by a desire to make a lasting impact on the lives of students, educators, and communities at large. It is a testament to the power of unity, collaboration, and the unwavering belief in the potential of every child. As you embark on this enlightening journey, we hope you discover new perspectives, ignite conversations, and gather the tools needed to reshape education in a profound and meaningful way.

So, dear reader, join us as we navigate the diverse landscape of educational transformation. Let us uncover the untapped potential, celebrate the unsung heroes, and forge a path towards a brighter, more inclusive future. Together, we will empower the MVPs of education—the dedicated teachers who leave an indelible mark on the hearts and minds of generations to come.

When discussing the importance of diversity in the educational system, it is essential to go beyond the common understanding of diversity, equity, and inclusion. From my perspective, diversity encompasses more than just gender representation; it extends to encompass race, economic backgrounds, life experiences, and even cultural lenses.

It is crucial to recognize that being a certain race or gender does not automatically qualify an individual to understand and connect with students facing unique challenges. For instance, being a black male does not inherently guarantee an innate ability to relate to the experiences of students in Chicago Public Schools on the south side. True diversity goes beyond surface-level characteristics; it requires a deep understanding of the complex factors that shape students' lives.

Let's consider the example of Cal, a black man from Charlotte, North Carolina, who now teaches in Memphis' Shelby County Schools. Cal is not just a product of his race or hometown; he brings a wealth of experiences as a former HBCU Student Government Association president and an individual who personally understands how the educational system impacts one's trajectory. His classroom approach is informed by his empathy, drawing on his own memories and first hand perspective. It is this ability to empathize, not merely sympathize, that truly reflects the essence of diversity in education.

When discussing diversity in the context of this book, we focus on race as a significant aspect. Of course, gender diversity is also important. However, what often goes unaddressed is the notion that being black does not automatically imply a shared understanding of the struggles faced by others. Similarly, growing up in a specific zip code does not guarantee an accurate comprehension of the daily challenges encountered by students in different neighborhoods.

Reflecting on historical references, we can draw parallels to slavery, where different perspectives emerged among black individuals. The House Negro and the Field Negro both identified as black, yet their experiences and outlooks were shaped by their unique circumstances. This historical context continues to influence education today, as life experiences and trauma play significant roles in shaping individuals' perspectives.

In essence, true diversity in education encompasses a broad range of factors, including life experiences, gender, race, and cultural lenses. It involves having individuals in the classroom who can genuinely empathize with the daily realities students face. By embracing these multifaceted aspects of diversity, we create a learning environment that acknowledges and addresses the complexities of students' lives, leading to more impactful educational experiences.

"The MVPs of Education" is a journey of discovery, empowerment, and transformation. It delves into the crucial role that diversity plays in shaping our educational landscape. As you have delved into the pages of this introduction, you have glimpsed the passion and purpose that drives our organization and the mission we share with other remarkable entities in this field.

But our story has just begun, and there is so much more to explore. In the chapters that lie ahead, you will encounter a wealth of strategies, resources, and best practices from diverse organizations that are making a profound impact on education. You will discover firsthand accounts of the triumphs and challenges faced by educators and administrators who have embraced the power of diversity. Each page is an invitation to unlock new possibilities, broaden your perspectives, and uncover innovative approaches that can revolutionize your own educational community.

So, dear reader, we invite you to journey with us further. Allow "The MVPs of Education" to be your guide, inspiring you to take bold steps toward creating a more inclusive and equitable educational system. Join us as we celebrate the extraordinary educators who leave an indelible mark on the lives of students, propelling them towards a future of endless possibilities.

Together, let us champion the cause of diversity, amplifying the voices and experiences that have been overlooked for far too long. Embrace this opportunity to collaborate, connect, and learn from the collective wisdom within these pages. As we navigate the chapters ahead, we are confident that you will be inspired, enlightened, and equipped with the tools to enact meaningful change.

Keep reading, dear reader, and let "The MVPs of Education" empower you to become an agent of transformation in the world of education.

Chapter One

Education As We Know It

"The function of education is to teach one to think intensively and to think critically. Intelligence plus character - that is the goal of true education." - Martin Luther King Jr.

I n 1954, a landmark ruling forever changed the landscape of education in the United States. The Brown vs. Board of Education decision, issued by the Supreme Court, declared that segregation in public schools was unconstitutional. This groundbreaking ruling set in motion a series of events that would shape the future of education and pave the way for desegregation efforts across the nation. However, amidst the celebrations and progress, the ruling had a profound impact on the black teacher workforce.

Prior to the Brown decision, black students were predominantly educated in segregated schools that had their own dedicated black teachers. These schools, while often under-resourced and facing discriminatory practices, served as pillars of the black community. They provided more than just education; they offered a sense of belonging, cultural identity, and a safe space for black students and educators alike.

The aftermath of the Brown ruling brought significant changes to the educational landscape. Many black schools were either shut down or integrated into previously all-white institutions. This resulted in a sharp decline in the number of black teachers across the country. According to a report by the National Education Association (NEA), the southern states saw their black teacher workforce diminish from 82,000 in 1955 to a mere 38,000 by 1965.

Integration, unfortunately, did not guarantee equal opportunities for black teachers. In many instances, these educators found themselves displaced from their positions or faced with systemic barriers that hindered their employment in integrated schools. Even for those who managed to secure teaching positions, discrimination persisted. They encountered lower salaries, limited support systems, and fewer chances for professional growth and advancement.

The consequences of this decline in the black teacher workforce were far-reaching, particularly for black students. Black teachers had long served as invaluable role models and mentors, providing inspiration and guidance to their students. Research has consistently shown that having teachers of the same race can yield positive academic and social-emotional outcomes, particularly for black students who benefit from the representation and cultural understanding that black teachers provide.

Despite the challenges they faced, black educators remained resilient and determined to fight for their rights and demand equal opportunities within the education system. Their unwavering commitment to educational equity has left an indelible mark on the pursuit of justice and equality in education. Today, the quest to recruit and retain black teachers continues, as the teaching profession remains one of the least diverse professions in the United States.

As we delve deeper into the MVPs (Most Valuable Process-es) of education, it is imperative to acknowledge the histor-ical context and the transformative impact of the Brown vs. Board of Education ruling. We must understand the struggles and triumphs of black educators, who have played a vital role in shaping the educational experiences of countless students. Through their perseverance and dedication, they have left an enduring legacy and an urgent call for a more diverse and inclusive teaching workforce.

In the chapters that follow, we will explore the critical processes that empower educators, promote educational eq-uity, and inspire meaningful change. By examining the re-cruitment, development, and retention of teachers, we aim to unravel the strategies that foster a more inclusive and impact-ful education system. Together, we will embark on a journey to elevate education to its highest potential and honor the invaluable contributions of educators from all walks of life.

In exploring the reasons behind the underrepresentation of Black people in the teaching profession, we encounter a range of factors that contribute to this disparity. Understanding these reasons is essential to addressing the issue and creating a more diverse and inclusive educational landscape. Here, we delve into some of the key factors that influence why Black individuals may not choose to pursue a career in education.

One prominent factor is the issue of low pay. Unfortunately, teachers' salaries often fall below those of other professions requiring similar levels of education and experience. This disparity in compensation can act as a deterrent for potential candidates, including many Black individuals, who may prioritize financial stability and security when considering career options.

Another significant obstacle is the burden of student loan debt. The cost of higher education and the resulting debt can pose a substantial barrier to entry for aspiring educators, particularly those from lower-income backgrounds. The prospect of shouldering significant financial obligations can dissuade individuals, including Black individuals, from pursuing a career in education.

The lack of representation within the education system is another critical factor. When Black individuals do not see themselves reflected in the teaching profession, it can create a sense of disconnection and isolation. Limited representation of Black teachers can dampen the appeal of the profession and hinder the formation of a diverse and inclusive educational environment. The absence of role models who share similar experiences and backgrounds can make the path to becoming an educator feel less attainable and fulfilling.

Perceived lack of support can also discourage Black individuals from pursuing teaching as a profession. They may perceive a lack of support from the education system itself and the broader society. This perception can be influenced by historical and ongoing systemic challenges faced by Black communities. When potential educators sense a lack of support, it diminishes their enthusiasm for entering.

The experiences of Black students in school play a crucial role in shaping their aspirations, including their desire to pursue a career in education. Let's explore some key factors that contribute to their hesitation:

Role models are essential, and when Black students don't see educators who look like them or understand their experiences, it can dampen their interest in pursuing a teaching career. The absence of positive role models in the profession leaves them without relatable figures to inspire and guide their own aspirations.

Negative experiences can be a significant deterrent. Black students who encounter negative interactions with educators or feel undervalued in the education system may hesitate to consider teaching as a career path. They may question whether they can truly make a positive impact or wonder if the profession welcomes individuals like them.

Low expectations can also hinder their inclination towards teaching. If Black students are not academically challenged or encouraged to pursue higher education, they may not see teaching as a viable option. Limited expectations can shape their perception of what they are capable of achieving, potentially closing doors to careers that require advanced degrees like teaching.

Burnout is a real concern. Black students who witness educators struggling with burnout or feeling unsupported may be dissuaded from entering a profession that appears stressful and lacking in support. Negative experiences during their own education journey may discourage them from pursuing a path that could potentially replicate those challenges.

It is crucial to recognize that the treatment of current Black students in school has lasting effects on their career aspirations, including their desire to become educators. By fostering fair treatment, respect, and inclusivity for all students, schools can create an environment that cultivates diverse teaching professionals. Providing positive role models, nurturing high expectations, and offering support throughout their educational journey can empower Black students to envision themselves as future educators and contribute to a more inclusive teaching profession.

As we reflect on the past of education and the challenges that persist in the present, it is evident that education as we know it is shaped by a complex interplay of historical events, social dynamics, and individual experiences. From the landmark Brown vs. Board of Education ruling to the underrepresentation of Black teachers and the barriers faced by Black students, our education system has both advanced and fallen short in its pursuit of equity and inclusivity.

We have explored the profound impact of desegregation efforts on the Black teacher workforce and the subsequent decline in representation. We have delved into the reasons why Black individuals may be deterred from pursuing careers in education, ranging from systemic barriers to negative experiences and perceptions. And we have recognized the critical role of positive role models, fair treatment, and high expectations in fostering a more diverse and inclusive teaching profession.

Yet, our journey does not end here. It is our collective responsibility as educators, administrators, policymakers, and advocates to continue striving for progress. We must address the disparities that persist, dismantle systemic barriers, and create environments where all students, regardless of their background, feel valued, empowered, and supported.

By embracing the power of representation, providing equitable opportunities, and cultivating inclusive spaces, we can inspire the next generation of educators, ensuring that they reflect the rich diversity of our society. Let us work together to redefine education, where every student has access to high-quality teaching, where every aspiring teacher feels welcomed and encouraged, and where the transformative potential of education is fully realized.

Education as we know it is a dynamic, evolving field. Let us seize the opportunity to shape it into a beacon of equality, empowerment, and excellence for all. Together, we can create a future where education truly becomes a gateway to limitless possibilities, unlocking the potential of every learner and nurturing a more inclusive society.

Chapter Reflection Questions:

Reflect on the historical context described in this chapter. How did the Brown vs. Board of Education ruling impact the black teacher workforce? What were the consequences of integration for black teachers?

_____

_____

_____

_____

_____

_____

Consider your own role in promoting diversity and inclusion in education. What steps can you take to create a more inclusive environment for students and educators? How can you contribute to the recruitment, development, and retention of diverse teachers?

_____

_____

_____

_____

Reflect on the significance of fair treatment, respect, and high expectations in shaping students' aspirations to become educators. How can schools foster a supportive and empowering environment that encourages all students to consider teaching as a viable and fulfilling career path?

Consider the broader impact of a transformed education system on society. How can a more diverse and inclusive teaching workforce contribute to a more inclusive and equitable society as a whole? What ripple effects can occur when students see themselves reflected in their teachers and feel empowered to achieve their full potential?

_____

_____

_____

_____

_____

_____

Chapter Reflection

Use the pages below to write your feelings or reflections from the chapter or take this time to write out your action plan to begin Finding Strategies for Combating the Teacher Shortage and Diversifying the Teacher Workforce

_____

_____

_____

_____

_____

_____

_____

_____

_____

_____

_____

_____

_____

_____

_____

Chapter Two

Our Hope For Education

"Education is the passport to the future, for tomorrow belongs to those who prepare for it today." - Malcolm X

In today's ever-evolving educational landscape, I find myself reimagining the very essence of what education should be. It's no longer confined to the traditional K-12 or P-16 pathways. Instead, my perspective has expanded to embrace a broader vision that transcends walls, buildings, and zip codes. I yearn for a complete transformation of the educational industry and sector as a whole.

To achieve this ambitious goal, we must dare to question the status quo and challenge conventional norms. It begins by fostering not only a diverse teacher workforce but also by considering vital aspects such as financial literacy and entrepreneurship. Surprisingly, even the largest school districts, like New York City's public school system, fail to require students to take courses in essential life skills like financial literacy. Education encompasses far more than standard curricula. It must equip students with the tools they need to navigate the complexities of the modern world.

My overarching aspiration is nothing short of dismantling and rebuilding the entire K-12 educational system from scratch. We must recognize that we are working with an outdated machine. Imagine restoring a beat-up, rusty 1964 Ford Mustang. You wouldn't simply replace the engine or add new tires. Instead, you'd embark on a frame-off rebuild, stripping the car down to its bare bones, revealing the true extent of necessary repairs.

Similarly, in education, we must break free from outdated practices and embark on a comprehensive overhaul. We need to assess every aspect of the system, including different curriculums, pathways, and educational approaches. By engaging in a frame-off rebuild, we can identify the underlying issues and reimagine a more effective and inclusive model.

Let's start with the engine—the driving force behind our educational system. From my perspective, the engine is none other than our dedicated teachers. They are the frontline educators, standing before classrooms filled with eager minds, ready to make a lasting impact. Their dedication, passion, and ability to connect with students are what truly set the educational machine in motion.

Just as an engine relies on a transmission to deliver power, teachers need support from other crucial components, such as parents. Building strong partnerships between educators and parents is essential for cultivating a positive and nurturing learning environment. Collaboration between these two forces can amplify the impact of education and ensure students receive the best possible support both inside and outside the classroom.

As we rebuild our educational "car," we must address the fundamental questions that underpin its purpose and effectiveness. Why are some students not learning? Why is there an overreliance on special education services? Why does the school-to-prison pipeline persist? Reflecting on landmark cases like Brown v. Board of Education, we can trace the historical impact of desegregation on the teaching profession in black and brown communities. We must learn from past experiences and rectify the systemic flaws that hinder equitable education for all.

In my vision, the journey towards a transformed educational system starts with empowering teachers. They are the catalysts for change, wielding the power to shape students' lives and futures. From classroom management to delivering high-quality instruction, teachers play a pivotal role in ensuring every student receives an exceptional education.

This vision, of course, reflects my personal opinions and aspirations. It is a call to action, urging us to recognize the pivotal role of teachers and the urgent need for a comprehensive educational transformation. By revitalizing our educational engine and reimagining every aspect of the system, we can lay the groundwork for a brighter, more equitable future.

So, let us embark on this adventure together—teachers, administrators, policymakers, parents, and students alike. With a shared commitment to rethinking and rebuilding, we can create an educational system that not only equips students with knowledge but also empowers them with the skills, resilence, and creativity needed to thrive in a rapidly changing world. Together, we can redefine the landscape of education and shape a future where every learner has the opportunity to excel.

The initial step towards transforming the educational system is to empower teachers and initiate a mindset shift within the profession. It's crucial to reeducate teachers about the diverse pathways available to them and encourage them to embrace new opportunities. In the current educational landscape, there exists an erroneous assumption that teachers should commit their entire careers to a single classroom, akin to Mrs. Brown, who has been teaching for 20 years. However, our generation thrives on change, seeking fresh experiences and exploring different avenues. It's unrealistic to expect teachers to remain in one position for decades when professionals in other industries freely move between companies, exploring diverse roles and embracing freelancing opportunities.

Imagine an employee at Google who, after three years, decides to work for Dell or transition to a career at TikTok or Instagram. It's common in technology-driven fields where human presence isn't the primary factor. Similarly, someone may work for Tesla before moving on to another automobile company. However, when it comes to teaching, the situation is unique because it involves human connections. Leaving a teaching position isn't merely about leaving a job; it also means parting ways with students and colleagues. This emotional attachment often makes it challenging for teachers to consider alternative paths.

Therefore, it's imperative to convey to educators that there are diverse opportunities available within the field of education. While teaching can be a starting point, it should be understood that it's not the only path to pursue. Unfortunately, this narrative remains untold, overshadowed by the emphasis on recruiting teachers. To attract and retain top talent, we must showcase the possibilities for growth, impact, and professional development within the education sector. If teachers know that they have the chance to grow within the organization, contribute as disruptors, and explore different roles and positions, they will be more inclined to join and stay committed.

Moreover, we need to debunk the misconception that the only way to contribute to education is through classroom teaching. Starting a charter school or establishing an educational firm are just a couple of examples of alternative paths one can take to make a substantial impact. Additionally, becoming an advocate for policy change or serving as an influential voice within the educational landscape are avenues that educators can explore. By broadening the narrative surrounding careers in education, we can attract a more diverse range of professionals and invigorate the system with fresh perspectives and ideas.

It is indeed possible to reimagine education and provide educators with the autonomy and opportunities they deserve. By fostering an environment where teachers feel supported, empowered, and equipped with the tools to navigate various career pathways, we can create a dynamic and innovative educational system. Let us embrace the notion that teaching is not solely confined to the classroom, but rather a springboard to numerous possibilities within the field of education. Together, we can cultivate a thriving educational ecosystem that attracts and retains passionate individuals committed to shaping the future of learning.

The significance of a diverse and inclusive teaching workforce cannot be overstated, especially when it comes to the presence of black educators. Extensive research has consistently shown the profound impact these educators have on students from all backgrounds, influencing their academic achievements, sense of belonging, and overall success.

Studies have shed light on the positive outcomes associated with black educators. For instance, research conducted by the National Bureau of Economic Research revealed that having just one black teacher during elementary school significantly increased the likelihood of black students pursuing higher education. These educators serve as powerful role models, inspiring students to reach for their aspirations and fostering a belief in their own potential.

Moreover, black educators have played a crucial role in narrowing the achievement gap.

The U.S. Department of Education's findings highlighted the disparities in disciplinary actions faced by black students compared to their white peers. However, when black students had black teachers, the disciplinary gap diminished significantly. Black educators implement culturally responsive teaching strategies, creating inclusive classrooms that reduce disciplinary disparities and promote a sense of belonging.

Beyond academic achievements, black educators also excel at promoting cultural competency and understanding among students from diverse backgrounds. Research published in the Journal of Negro Education demonstrated that exposure to black educators increased students' cultural awareness and empathy towards their peers. This enhanced understanding of different cultures and perspectives equips students to thrive in a society that embraces diversity.

The positive impact of black educators extends to students' emotional well-being. Students who learn from black educators report feeling valued, supported, and empowered. The Journal of Educational Research highlighted that black students with black teachers exhibit higher self-esteem and a stronger sense of cultural identity. These factors significantly contribute to improved student engagement and motivation.

Recognizing the importance of this issue, various initiatives and organizations have emerged to encourage and support the recruitment and retention of black educators. Programs like Call Me MISTER (Mentors Instructing Students Toward Effective Role Models) and the Black Male Teacher Initiative have successfully attracted and trained black educators, addressing the underrepresentation within schools.

In conclusion, the presence of black educators in our educational system has proven to be transformative. From academic achievements to fostering inclusive environments and empowering students, their influence reaches far beyond the confines of the classroom. It is imperative that we continue to champion diversity, equity, and inclusion in our teaching workforce, ensuring that students from all backgrounds have access to exceptional educators who can positively shape their educational journeys and prepare them for a diverse and interconnected world.

The presence of black educators in the United States offers a multitude of benefits for students, encompassing academic achievement, disciplinary equity, cultural awareness, and identity development. Recognizing the significance of diversity and actively supporting efforts to increase representation, schools can foster a more inclusive and equitable educational environment, empowering every student to unlock their full potential.

The advantages of a diverse teacher workforce, particularly with increased representation of black educators, are far-reaching and have a transformative impact on students. One of the most significant benefits lies in the realm of academic achievement. Extensive research has consistently shown that black students who learn from black teachers exhibit enhanced academic performance, with higher graduation rates and a greater likelihood of attending college. The presence of black educators serves as a powerful source of inspiration and motivation for black students, as they witness firsthand positive role models who exemplify success and the pursuit of dreams.

Beyond academic success, the inclusion of black educators in schools plays a crucial role in reducing disciplinary disparities. Black students often face disproportionately high rates of disciplinary actions and suspensions compared to their white counterparts. However, with black teachers who possess a deep understanding of the cultural nuances and challenges faced by black students, disciplinary gaps can be significantly reduced. Black educators bring a unique perspective and a wealth of experience that allows them to establish connections with students, address their specific needs, and create an inclusive and supportive classroom environment.

Another advantage lies in the promotion of cultural awareness and understanding among students from diverse backgrounds. By incorporating the experiences and perspectives of black educators, classrooms become spaces where students can learn from and engage with different cultures, fostering empathy and empathy towards their peers. This increased cultural awareness equips students with valuable skills for navigating an increasingly diverse society, encouraging respect, acceptance, and collaboration.

Moreover, the presence of black educators has a profound impact on students' self-esteem and sense of belonging. Black students who have black teachers often report feeling valued, supported, and empowered within the educational setting. This nurturing environment positively influences their self-perception, boosts their confidence, and strengthens their overall sense of identity and belonging. As a result, students are more engaged and motivated in their learning journey, leading to improved educational outcomes.

By embracing the advantages of a diverse teacher workforce, schools can create a transformative educational experience for all students. The integration of black educators not only addresses the disparities and challenges faced by black students but also fosters a culture of inclusivity and equity that benefits the entire student body. These educators serve as catalysts for positive change, breaking down barriers, promoting understanding, and cultivating acceptance among individuals from diverse racial and ethnic backgrounds.

In the pursuit of an educational system that honors diversity and promotes equal opportunities for all, the presence of more black educators represents a significant step forward. By recognizing the immense value they bring to the classroom, we can create a future where students thrive, empowered by the support, guidance, and inspiration of teachers who reflect their own unique experiences and backgrounds.

As we embark on the journey of transforming our educational system, we must recognize the pivotal role of teachers and the need for a mindset shift within the profession. By reeducating teachers about the diverse pathways available to them, we can unlock a world of possibilities within the field of education. It is time to break free from the notion that teaching is a lifelong commitment to a single classroom, and instead embrace the idea of growth, change, and exploration.

Let us shatter the traditional mold and empower educators to be pioneers, disruptors, and agents of change. By showcasing the various avenues for professional development and impact, we can attract a diverse range of talent to the field of education. Just as individuals in other industries freely move between companies and explore different roles, teachers too should have the opportunity to embark on new adventures, make meaningful contributions, and continue to grow throughout their careers.

Furthermore, it is essential to dispel the belief that teaching is the only way to make a difference in education. By highlighting alternative paths such as starting charter schools, establishing educational firms, advocating for policy change, or becoming influential voices in the field, we can expand the possibilities for impact and innovation.

Together, let us reimagine education as a dynamic and ever-evolving ecosystem. Let us provide teachers with the autonomy, support, and resources they need to navigate diverse career pathways. By doing so, we can create an educational system that nurtures lifelong learners, embraces change, and prepares students for the challenges and opportunities of the future.

The road ahead may be challenging, but with a collective commitment to transform the educational landscape, we can build a brighter future for our students and educators alike. Let us embark on this transformative journey, dismantling outdated structures and embracing a new era of education. The possibilities are boundless, and together, we can reshape the landscape of learning for generations to come.

Chapter Reflection Questions:

What is your perspective on the current state of education and its limitations? How do you envision a broader and more inclusive educational landscape?

_____

_____

_____

_____

_____

_____

Reflecting on the role of teachers as the driving force behind the educational system, what qualities and attributes do you believe make a teacher impactful and effective?

_____

_____

_____

_____

_____

_____

How can strong partnerships between educators and parents contribute to creating a positive and nurturing learning en-

vironment? In what ways can collaboration between these two forces amplify the impact of education?

_____

_____

_____

_____

_____

_____

What initiatives and programs exist to support the recruitment and retention of black educators? How can these initiatives be expanded to address the underrepresentation of black educators in schools?

_____

_____

_____

_____

_____

_____

How can a mindset shift within the teaching profession contribute to the transformation of the educational system? What possibilities and opportunities can arise from reeducating teachers about diverse pathways and embracing growth, change, and exploration?

_____

_____

_____

_____

_____

_____

Chapter Reflection

Use the pages below to write your feelings or reflections from the chapter or take this time to write out your action plan to begin Finding Strategies for Combating the Teacher Shortage and Diversifying the Teacher Workforce

_____

_____

_____

_____

_____

_____

_____

_____

_____

_____

_____

_____

_____

_____

_____

Chapter Three

Educational MVPs - Most Valuable Processes

"Education is the fundamental method of social progress and reform." - W.E.B. Dubois

As a former educator in a charter school, I have gained valuable insights into the experiences of educators and the educational system. When considering the most valuable processes for schools, it is important to recognize that certain aspects remain constant across different locations and contexts. The fundamentals of education, such as mathematics, language arts, and science, have consistent standards regardless of the city or state. However, when delving into the most valuable processes from a teacher's perspective, we must acknowledge that it begins with opening the doors of education.

Creating effective curricula, implementing teaching practices, and fostering community development all stem from the foundation of education. As charter school operators or new school principals, it is essential to prioritize the identification, cultivation, development, and retention of talent. In many ways, this parallels the importance of a head coach in a sports franchise. While players may change, the coach plays a vital role in guiding, teaching, and shaping the team. Similarly, in education, the teachers serve as the core principles who impact the students, parents, and community.

Hence, the first process to consider when reflecting on the most valuable processes (MVPs) in education is talent recruitment, development, and retention. It is crucial to have dynamic and skilled teachers who can engage and inspire students. While implementing innovative teaching techniques and incorporating technology are valuable, it is the presence of exceptional educators that truly drives the educational experience. When charter school founders outline their plans, it is essential to have a solid recruitment strategy in place, ensuring that the right talent is brought on board.

By focusing on talent as the MVP of education, we can initiate a paradigm shift and truly impact and transform the educational landscape. Teachers are the driving force behind student success, and investing in their recruitment, development, and retention is a key starting point. While bells and whistles like project-based learning, close reading techniques, and integrated technology have their place, they are most effective when paired with dynamic teachers who possess the ability to connect with and inspire students.

When examining the MVPs in education, it becomes clear that it all begins with teachers. They are the linchpin of the educational process and have the power to shape the future. By prioritizing talent recruitment, development, and retention, schools can lay a strong foundation for effective teaching and create a positive and transformative educational experience for all students.

As we delve deeper into the discussion of the most valuable processes (MVPs) in education, the pivotal role of teachers becomes increasingly evident. While educational standards and subject matters may remain consistent, it is the quality and dedication of the teaching staff that truly determines the impact and success of a school. Therefore, prioritizing talent recruitment, development, and retention emerges as a key aspect in fostering an exceptional educational environment.

To establish an effective and thriving educational institution, the first step is identifying and attracting talented individuals who possess the passion and skills required to educate and inspire students. This process goes beyond a mere job posting; it involves actively seeking out individuals who embody the qualities of an exceptional educator. School leaders must engage in strategic recruitment efforts, targeting both experienced professionals and promising emerging talent. By casting a wide net and embracing diversity, schools can tap into a rich pool of educators with unique perspectives and experiences, thereby enhancing the overall learning environment.

However, identifying talent is just the beginning. Once teachers are brought on board, it is essential to invest in their ongoing development. Effective professional development programs provide teachers with the tools, resources, and support necessary to continuously grow and refine their instructional practices. These programs should not only focus on enhancing subject knowledge but also emphasize pedagogical skills, classroom management strategies, and the integration of innovative teaching methods. By offering opportunities for professional growth and creating a culture of continuous learning, schools can empower their teachers to deliver engaging and effective instruction that meets the evolving needs of students.

Retaining talented educators is equally crucial in building a successful school community. A supportive and nurturing environment that values and acknowledges the contributions of teachers is essential for teacher satisfaction and longevity. School leaders must create a positive workplace culture that fosters collaboration, open communication, and professional autonomy. Providing teachers with opportunities for leadership roles, mentorship programs, and avenues for professional advancement not only boosts their morale but also establishes a sense of loyalty and commitment to the school's mission.

Moreover, recognizing the importance of teacher well-being and work-life balance is vital for retaining talent. Educators often face significant challenges and demands in their profession, from long working hours to emotional labor.

Offering comprehensive support systems, including mental health resources, wellness programs, and flexible work arrangements, can help alleviate these pressures and contribute to teacher retention.

By prioritizing talent recruitment, development, and retention as essential MVPs, schools can cultivate a vibrant educational ecosystem that nurtures the growth and success of both students and educators. Exceptional teachers serve as catalysts for change, inspiring students to reach their full potential and shaping the future of society. Therefore, it is incumbent upon school leaders and education policymakers to invest in these MVPs and establish a robust framework that values and supports the teaching profession.

While educational standards and subject matters form the foundation of education, it is the quality of teachers that brings these elements to life. Talent recruitment, development, and retention serve as crucial MVPs, driving the success of educational institutions. By strategically identifying and attracting talented individuals, offering continuous professional development, and fostering a supportive work environment, schools can create a transformative educational experience that prepares students for a dynamic and diverse world. Ultimately, investing in teachers as the MVPs of education is an investment in the future of our students and society as a whole.

To more effectively recruit, retain, and develop teachers, it is crucial to follow a step-by-step process that aligns with the goals and needs of the educational institution. The journey begins with a thorough self-audit and gap identification. Principals, HR directors, or superintendents must take a close look at their school system and identify areas that require improvement. By understanding the direction in which they want the district or university School of Education program to progress, leaders can determine the type of talent they need to bring into the environment.

Once the gaps have been identified, the focus shifts to talent recruitment. School leaders must actively seek out and attract the desired talent. This can be done through various methods, such as directly recruiting from teacher talent pools or alternative teacher pathway programs. In some cases, the talent pool may be limited, prompting the need to cultivate talent from within the organization. Developing talent internally involves strategically nurturing individuals who show potential and providing them with opportunities for growth and advancement. By investing in the development of their own talent, schools can ensure a sustainable pipeline of skilled educators.

The next step in the process is talent development. It is essential to provide ongoing support and training to teachers to enhance their skills and knowledge. This can be achieved through professional growth programs, pedagogical training, and the integration of innovative teaching practices. Collaborating with local universities or establishing partnerships with educational programs can further support the development of talent. By equipping teachers with the necessary tools and knowledge, schools create a culture of excellence and ensure that educators are well-prepared to deliver high-quality instruction.

Retaining exceptional teachers is crucial for the long-term success of an educational institution. The step of talent retention requires a focus on employee satisfaction and well-being. Schools must offer competitive compensation packages, opportunities for professional advancement, and supportive work environments. Fostering partnerships and providing necessary resources are also vital in creating an environment that values and supports teachers. Recognizing the achievements and contributions of educators helps establish a sense of loyalty and commitment. By prioritizing talent retention, schools establish stability, continuity, and a positive school culture.

Moreover, the process of effective teacher recruitment, retention, and development is not just limited to the immediate goals of the institution. It should also include a focus on educator pathways. Educating individuals about the various career progression opportunities within the organization is crucial. By clearly outlining the potential growth and development prospects, schools can attract motivated individuals who are eager to advance their careers in education. This pathway approach also aids in talent retention, as educators can envision their long-term trajectory and work towards their professional goals within the organization. By nurturing and supporting their aspirations, schools create a pipeline of talent and enhance the overall success of the educational system.

In shaping these step-by-step processes, educational institutions can draw inspiration from successful models like Call Me Mister, Center For Black Teacher Development, National Center For Teacher Residences, Brothers Empowered to

Teach and corporate entities with robust talent development strategies. By prioritizing talent and providing the necessary support, schools can cultivate a highly skilled and motivated workforce that positively impacts student achievement and contributes to the overall improvement of education. Ultimately, this approach leads to a culture of continuous growth, where educators are empowered to reach their full potential, resulting in enhanced learning experiences for students.

The journey of effective teacher recruitment, retention, and development is a transformative one for educational institutions. By following a deliberate step-by-step process, schools can create a dynamic and supportive environment that attracts, nurtures, and retains exceptional educators. It begins with a self-audit, identifying the gaps that need to be filled and envisioning the direction the institution wants to take. From there, the focus shifts to talent recruitment, whether it be from external sources or through internal growth programs. Developing the identified talent is a continuous effort that involves providing professional development opportunities and fostering partnerships with universities and other educational programs.

Retaining teachers is of utmost importance, and this can be achieved by prioritizing employee satisfaction, offering competitive compensation, and creating a supportive work culture. By investing in the growth and well-being of educators, schools cultivate a sense of loyalty and commitment that contributes to long-term success. Additionally, the notion of educator pathways plays a crucial role in the process. By educating individuals about the various career progression opportunities within the organization, schools can attract ambitious individuals who are eager to make a difference in education.

As we embark on this journey of recruitment, development, and retention, let us draw inspiration from successful models and adapt their strategies to our unique contexts. By prioritizing talent and providing the necessary support, we can create a nurturing environment that empowers educators to thrive. Together, we can build a culture of continuous growth, where teachers are valued as the catalysts of positive change and students reap the benefits of their expertise and dedication.

Remember, the impact of effective teacher recruitment, retention, and development goes far beyond the walls of our institutions. It ripples through generations, shaping the future of education and society as a whole. So let us embrace this journey with enthusiasm, determination, and a shared commitment to excellence. Together, we can unleash the full potential of our educational system and ensure a brighter future for all.

Chapter Reflection Questions:

How well do you currently understand the gaps and needs within your educational institution? What steps can you take to conduct a thorough self-audit and identify areas for improvement?

_____

_____

_____

_____

_____

_____

What strategies can you implement to enhance your talent recruitment efforts? How can you leverage external talent pools, alternative teacher pathway programs, or internal development programs to attract exceptional educators?

_____

_____

_____

_____

_____

_____

How can you create a culture of continuous professional development and growth within your institution? What resources and opportunities can you provide to support the ongoing development of your teachers?

_____

_____

_____

_____

_____

Reflect on your current practices for teacher retention. What measures are in place to ensure high employee satisfaction? How can you enhance compensation, work culture, and support systems to improve teacher retention rates?

_____

_____

_____

_____

_____

_____

What is your vision for educator pathways within your institution? How can you educate and empower individuals about the various career progression opportunities available to them? What steps can you take to support their growth and advancement?

_____

_____

_____

_____

_____

_____

Chapter Activity:

- Implement a Talent Recruitment Strategy Session

- Gather a team of key stakeholders, including administrators, department heads, and human resources personnel, to discuss talent recruitment strategies.

- Begin by conducting a comprehensive analysis of the current recruitment practices and identifying any gaps or areas for improvement.

- Brainstorm creative and innovative ideas for attracting top talent, considering both external and internal recruitment sources.

- Develop a recruitment plan that includes clear goals, target audiences, recruitment channels, and timelines.

- Assign specific responsibilities to team members and establish accountability measures to ensure the implementation of the recruitment plan.

- Evaluate and refine the recruitment strategies periodically based on feedback, results, and evolving needs.

- Continuously monitor and assess the effectiveness of recruitment efforts, making adjustments as necessary to optimize outcomes.

Chapter Reflection

Use the pages below to write your feelings or reflections from the chapter or take this time to write out your action plan to begin Finding Strategies for Combating the Teacher Shortage and Diversifying the Teacher Workforce

_____

_____

_____

_____

_____

_____

_____

_____

_____

_____

_____

_____

_____

_____

_____

Chapter Four

Identifying Prospects | Recruitment

"The best teachers are those who show you where to look but don't tell you what to see." - Alexandra K. Trenfor

I n the quest for excellence in education, it is essential to identify and recruit top prospects for teaching and educational leadership positions. Just as top professional championship franchises in sports use strategic methods to identify talented athletes, schools can adopt similar practices to attract exceptional educators. This chapter explores the various strategies employed by successful sports franchises and how they can be adapted to the field of education.

We will delve into effective recruitment strategies, including building relationships with institutions, offering incentives, partnering with community organizations, and utilizing employee referrals. Additionally, we will explore the significance of diversity in the workforce and its impact on students and school communities. By implementing these strategies and embracing a proactive approach, schools can cultivate a strong and diverse talent pool, ensuring the delivery of high-quality education to every student.

Looking into the not-so-distant future of education, the year 2024 paints a sobering picture. A staggering 1.9 million teacher vacancies are projected across the United States, leaving a staggering 45.6 million students without the guidance and support of a certified teacher in their classrooms. Amidst this alarming situation, the underrepresentation of Black teachers persists, with their numbers comprising less than 10% of the overall teacher workforce, despite students of color accounting for a significant 51% of the student population.

In the face of such challenges, it becomes imperative to adopt proactive strategies for identifying prospects and recruiting talented individuals who can shape the future of education. Let us delve into some key approaches that can transform the recruitment landscape and foster a diverse and inclusive educational environment.

Firstly, building meaningful relationships with Historically Black Colleges and Universities (HBCUs) and other minority-serving institutions is a crucial step. These institutions embody a rich reservoir of untapped potential, brimming with bright minds eager to make a difference in the lives of students. By establishing robust partnerships with HBCUs and minority-serving institutions, school districts can forge powerful connections that open doors to diverse candidates who possess the passion, knowledge, and cultural understanding necessary to effectively engage with students from diverse backgrounds. Engaging in collaborative efforts, such as career fairs, mentorship programs, and targeted outreach initiatives, can cultivate a strong and dynamic pipeline of talented individuals ready to embark on a rewarding journey in education.

Secondly, recognizing the value of attracting Black educators, school districts should consider offering enticing incentives to make the profession even more appealing. The
journey of a teacher often involves uprooting their lives and
embracing new communities. By providing signing bonuses,
relocation assistance, and housing allowances, school districts
can ease the financial burden of this transition, making it
more feasible and attractive for Black educators to join their
ranks. Such initiatives demonstrate a genuine commitment to
supporting and valuing diverse educators, ensuring that they
feel valued and appreciated from the very beginning of their
professional journey.

Additionally, forging partnerships with community organizations that champion education and diversity can be a
game-changer in the recruitment process. These organizations serve as vital bridges between schools and the wider
community, possessing deep insights into local talent pools
and networks. Collaborating with community organizations
enables school districts to tap into their expertise and connections, enabling the identification and connection with talented Black educators. Furthermore, these partnerships can
provide ongoing support, mentorship programs, and valu-

able resources to new Black educators, nurturing their professional growth and fostering a sense of belonging in their chosen career path.

As we embark on this journey of identifying prospects and recruiting diverse talent, let us remember that this endeavor is not merely an administrative task but an ethical imperative. By actively seeking out and nurturing Black educators, we can bridge the gap between the underrepresentation of Black teachers and the diverse student population they serve. Each recruitment effort is an opportunity to build a teaching workforce that mirrors the rich tapestry of our student body, providing role models and mentors who understand and champion the unique experiences and challenges faced by students of color.

In the chapters that follow, we will delve deeper into strategies for retaining and developing teachers, fostering inclusive and supportive environments, and redefining education as a transformative force. Together, let us embrace these recruitment practices as an empowering journey toward a more equitable and enriching educational landscape, where every student is empowered to thrive and succeed. Our collective commitment to diversity and inclusion will pave the way for a brighter future, where education becomes a catalyst for positive change in the lives of all students.

Recruiting Black educators to school districts in urban communities can be a challenging task, but there are several strategies that can be employed to increase diversity in faculty. These strategies can be implemented by school districts, charter school networks, or private school systems. Here are some effective recruitment strategies:

Firstly, building strong relationships with Historically Black Colleges and Universities (HBCUs) and other minority-serving institutions is essential. These institutions are renowned for nurturing a diverse pool of talented candidates for teaching positions. By establishing partnerships with HBCUs and minority-serving institutions, school districts can tap into this talent pool and actively recruit and hire Black educators who bring unique perspectives and experiences to the classroom.

In addition to forging connections with colleges and universities, targeted advertising and marketing campaigns can play a pivotal role in attracting Black educators. Utilizing platforms such as social media, job boards, and other relevant channels, school districts can reach a wider audience and highlight the benefits of teaching in urban communities. By showcasing the diversity of the school district and the inclusive environment it fosters, these campaigns can pique the interest of Black educators seeking impactful teaching opportunities.

To further entice Black educators, offering incentives can make the school district more appealing. Signing bonuses, relocation assistance, and housing allowances can help alleviate the financial burdens associated with transitioning to a new community. By providing these incentives, school districts demonstrate their commitment to supporting and valuing diverse educators from the outset, making the prospect of joining the district more enticing.

Professional development opportunities are another effective recruitment strategy. By offering ongoing professional growth and advancement programs, school districts can not only retain Black educators but also attract others who are seeking opportunities for career development. These opportunities can include mentorship programs, leadership training, and specialized workshops tailored to meet the needs of Black educators.

Partnering with community organizations that prioritize education and diversity is yet another powerful strategy. These organizations can serve as valuable allies in identifying and recruiting Black educators. Additionally, they can offer support, resources, and networking opportunities for new Black educators, helping them navigate their careers with confidence.

Employee referrals can also be a fruitful avenue for recruitment. By fostering a culture that values diversity and inclusion, school districts can encourage current employees to refer Black educators to the district. This can be incentivized or simply nurtured through a workplace environment that actively seeks to promote diversity.

Attending job fairs and conferences that focus on diversity and education is an effective means of networking with potential candidates. These events provide opportunities to meet and connect with Black educators who are actively seeking teaching positions. By participating in these gatherings, school districts can showcase their commitment to diversity and engage directly with prospective educators.

In conclusion, recruiting Black educators in urban communities requires a proactive and intentional approach. By building relationships with institutions, employing targeted advertising, offering incentives, providing professional development opportunities, partnering with community organizations, leveraging employee referrals, and participating in relevant events, school districts can attract and retain diverse talent that will contribute to the success of their students. These strategies lay the foundation for fostering a vibrant and inclusive educational environment where students can thrive and reach their full potential.

In the quest to identify top prospects for teaching and educational leadership positions, schools can adopt effective strategies that mirror the methods employed by top professional championship franchises in the sports industry. These strategies encompass a range of initiatives aimed at attracting and selecting the most promising candidates. By implementing these approaches, schools can ensure they build a talented and diverse workforce capable of meeting the evolving needs of their students.

One powerful strategy involves organizing recruitment events, such as job fairs or career days, which provide platforms for schools to engage with potential teacher candidates. These events facilitate face-to-face interactions, enabling schools to assess candidates' qualifications, experience, and passion for education. By actively participating in recruitment events, schools can showcase their unique culture, educational philosophy, and commitment to student success, thereby attracting candidates who align with their values and objectives.

Furthermore, internship programs have proven to be invaluable in identifying top prospects in the field of education. By offering aspiring educators the opportunity to gain hands-on experience in the classroom, schools can assess candidates' teaching style, classroom management skills, and ability to connect with students. Internships provide a fertile ground for candidates to demonstrate their dedication, adaptability, and potential for growth within the educational setting. This first hand exposure allows schools to evaluate a candidate's ability to effectively engage students, deliver impactful lessons, and foster a positive and inclusive learning environment.

In addition to internships, schools can establish professional development programs as a means of identifying individuals with leadership potential. These programs provide ongoing training and support to current staff members, fostering continuous growth and improvement. Through professional development initiatives, schools can observe the dedication, initiative, and willingness of educators to embrace new methodologies and assume leadership roles. Identifying staff members who exhibit these qualities can lead to their progression into positions of greater responsibility, such as mentorship roles or administrative positions, ensuring the cultivation of a strong pipeline of future educational leaders.

To expand their reach and access a broader talent pool, schools can implement referral programs. These programs encourage current staff members, alumni, and community members to refer potential candidates who may possess the desired qualifications and characteristics. By leveraging existing networks, schools can tap into diverse communities and identify promising individuals who may not have considered a career in education or been aware of specific job opportunities. Referral programs foster a sense of shared responsibility and engagement within the school community, strengthening connections and promoting collaboration.

By investing in recruitment, training, and development, schools can build a robust and dynamic workforce that meets the diverse needs of their students. Through effective recruitment events, internship programs, professional development initiatives, and referral programs, schools can identify top prospects who possess the passion, skills, and dedication necessary to thrive in teaching and educational leadership positions. These strategic approaches not only contribute to the quality of education but also foster an inclusive and vibrant school culture that empowers students and cultivates their potential.

Schools can adopt a range of strategies to identify top prospects for teaching and educational leadership positions. By mirroring the methods used by top professional championship franchises in sports, schools can attract and select talented individuals who are passionate about education and dedicated to student success. Through recruitment events, internship programs, professional development initiatives, and referral programs, schools can create a strong and diverse workforce that meets the evolving needs of their students. Investing in these strategies not only enhances the quality of education but also fosters a vibrant and inclusive school community. By prioritizing the identification and cultivation of top prospects, schools ensure a brighter future for their students and the field of education as a whole.

Chapter Reflection Questions:

How can the strategies used by top professional championship franchises in sports be adapted and applied to the field of education for identifying top teaching prospects?

_____

_____

_____

_____

_____

_____

Why is it important for schools to have a diverse workforce of talented educators? How does it benefit both students and the school community?

_____

_____

_____

_____

_____

_____

Reflect on your own experiences as a student. Have you ever encountered a teacher or educational leader who stood out to you as exceptional? What qualities and characteristics did they possess?

_____

_____

_____

_____

_____

_____

Consider the strategies discussed in this chapter. Which ones do you find most intriguing or effective in identifying top prospects for teaching and educational leadership positions? Why?

_____

_____

_____

_____

_____

_____

Chapter Student Activity:

Imagine you are a school administrator tasked with identifying top prospects for teaching positions in your school district. Design a recruitment event or program that incorporates the strategies discussed in this chapter. Create a detailed plan outlining the objectives, activities, and target audience for the event or program. Consider how you will promote diversity, attract talented candidates, and ensure a fair selection process. Present your plan to the class, highlighting the reasons behind your choices and the expected impact on the school community. Engage in a discussion with your classmates to exchange ideas and receive feedback on your recruitment strategy.

Chapter Reflection

Use the pages below to write your feelings or reflections from the chapter or take this time to write out your action plan to begin Finding Strategies for Combating the Teacher Shortage and Diversifying the Teacher Workforce

_____

_____

_____

_____

_____

_____

_____

_____

_____

_____

_____

_____

_____

_____

_____

_____

_____

_____

_____

_____

_____

_____

_____

_____

_____

_____

_____

_____

_____

_____

_____

_____

_____

Chapter Five

Developing Talent

"A good teacher can inspire hope, ignite the imagination, and instill a love of learning." - Brad Henry

I n our unwavering pursuit of educational excellence, it is imperative to confront the challenges surrounding the development of talented teachers, particularly those from underrepresented backgrounds. This chapter delves into the paramount importance of cultivating a diverse teaching force and explores the intricate barriers that impede the progress of black students seeking careers in education. We will closely examine the current educational landscape, acknowledging the data from the National Center for Education Statistics

(NCES) that illuminates the enrollment of black students in education programs. However, it is crucial to recognize and confront the multifaceted obstacles that deter these aspiring educators from completing their programs and realizing their aspirations within the teaching profession.

Furthermore, schools grapple with the intricate task of developing teachers for a plethora of reasons. Limited resources and funding, particularly in low-income communities, present a considerable challenge in implementing effective teacher development programs that equip educators with the necessary skills and knowledge to thrive in their roles. Moreover, the persistently high rates of teacher turnover pose a significant hurdle, hindering schools' efforts to retain and cultivate a pool of talented educators. This constant turnover not only disrupts the stability of classrooms but also hampers the collective growth and progress of the teaching staff.

In addition, the limited support and mentorship available to teachers further compound the challenges they face. Adequate guidance and ongoing mentorship play a pivotal role in the professional development of teachers, enabling them to refine their instructional skills and achieve optimal student outcomes. Without robust support systems in place, educators may struggle to navigate the complexities of the profession and unlock their full potential.

Another salient issue faced by schools is the dearth of diversity within their teaching staff. This lack of representation presents significant obstacles to delivering culturally responsive instruction and addressing the unique needs of students from diverse backgrounds. It is imperative to acknowledge that students thrive in environments where they see themselves reflected in their teachers and have access to role models who understand and value their experiences.

Recognizing the urgent need for innovative approaches to combat the teacher shortage and cultivate a more diverse teaching force, research substantiates the pivotal role of representation in promoting academic success, particularly for historically marginalized students. The presence of teachers who share common experiences and backgrounds can provide a sense of belonging, instill confidence, and foster positive academic outcomes. Therefore, attracting and retaining teachers of color, specifically black teachers, is an urgent priority within the education profession.

To address this issue, innovative approaches to teacher development must be firmly rooted in diversity, equity, and inclusion. One promising strategy is the "grow your own" model, which identifies potential teachers from within the school or local community and provides them with the necessary support and resources to embark on a journey towards becoming certified educators. This approach capitalizes on the familiarity these aspiring teachers have with the school's culture, values, and instructional practices, fostering a profound commitment to serving their communities.

In addition to the "grow your own" model, targeted support and mentorship for black teachers can be instrumental in their professional growth and success. Tailored professional development opportunities that emphasize culturally responsive instruction, trauma-informed teaching, and anti-racist practices empower these educators to navigate the unique challenges they may encounter within the profession. Furthermore, mentorship programs and networking initiatives that connect black teachers create a supportive community where experiences, knowledge, and expertise can be shared, fostering an environment of growth and collaboration.

Developing a more diverse teaching force is an urgent imperative for addressing the teacher shortage and improving outcomes for all students. By embracing innovative approaches to teacher development that prioritize diversity, equity, and inclusion, we can attract and retain more black teachers, ultimately leading to positive educational outcomes for students from all backgrounds. Let us embark on a transformative journey as we explore these strategies that cultivate talent, foster inclusivity, and propel our educational institutions towards a brighter future.

It is imperative to confront the challenges surrounding the development of talented teachers, particularly those from underrepresented backgrounds. This chapter delves into the paramount importance of cultivating a diverse teaching force and explores the intricate barriers that impede the progress of black students seeking careers in education. We will closely examine the current educational landscape, acknowledging the data from the National Center for Education Statistics (NCES) that illuminates the enrollment of black students in education programs. However, it is crucial to recognize and confront the multifaceted obstacles that deter these aspiring educators from completing their programs and realizing their aspirations within the teaching profession.

Starting Young: Creating a Talent Pipeline

One key approach to developing a diverse teaching force is to start cultivating talent at a young age. By focusing efforts on identifying and nurturing promising individuals early on, schools can lay the foundation for a strong talent pipeline. This proactive strategy involves engaging with students in elementary and secondary schools, exposing them to the joys and rewards of teaching, and providing mentorship and guidance throughout their educational journey.

Educational Outreach Programs: Schools and educational organizations can collaborate with local schools to implement educational outreach programs. These programs can include classroom visits, workshops, and interactive activities designed to spark students' interest in teaching. By fostering a positive and engaging experience, young individuals can begin to envision themselves as future educators.

Career Exploration Opportunities: Offering career exploration opportunities, such as internships, shadowing programs, and summer camps, can provide young students with firsthand exposure to the teaching profession. These immersive experiences allow them to observe and participate in classroom settings, interact with educators, and gain valuable insights into the joys and challenges of being a teacher.

Mentorship Initiatives: Establishing mentorship programs that pair aspiring educators with experienced teachers can provide ongoing support and guidance. Mentors can offer valuable advice, share their own teaching experiences, and help students navigate the educational pathway towards becoming certified teachers.

Grow Your Own: Cultivating Talent within the Community

Another effective strategy for developing a diverse teaching force is the "grow your own" approach. This model involves identifying potential teachers from within the school or local community and providing them with the necessary support and resources to pursue careers in education. By harnessing the unique strengths and perspectives of individuals already embedded within the community, schools can create a teaching workforce that reflects the diversity of the student population.

Talent Identification: Schools can actively identify individuals within the community who possess the qualities and potential to become exceptional educators. This can be done through teacher recommendations, community referrals, or targeted recruitment efforts. By recognizing the inherent talents and passion of these individuals, schools can embark on a journey of nurturing and developing their teaching skills.

Scholarships and Financial Support: Financial barriers can often hinder aspiring educators from pursuing teaching careers. To address this, schools can offer scholarships, grants, or financial aid programs specifically tailored to support individuals from underrepresented backgrounds. By easing the financial burden, more individuals can access the education and training necessary to become licensed teachers.

Mentorship and Professional Development: Once identified, it is essential to provide ongoing mentorship and professional development opportunities to aspiring teachers. Mentorship programs can pair these individuals with experienced educators who can guide them through their educational journey, offer advice, and share best practices. Additionally, tailored professional development programs can equip them with the necessary instructional strategies, cultural competency skills, and knowledge to succeed in the classroom.

Partnering with Community Organizations: Collaborative Efforts for Talent Development

Schools cannot tackle the task of developing a diverse teaching force alone. Partnering with community organizations that focus on education and diversity is a critical step in cultivating talent and creating a supportive network for aspiring educators. These partnerships can provide valuable resources, support systems, and advocacy for individuals pursuing teaching careers. Additionally, partnering with organizations such as Black Leaders Organizing Communities (BLOC), He is Me Institute, or Tennessee Educators of Color Alliance and allow these community based organizations to assist you in building transformational relationships in order to empower black leaders with the tools, training and resources needed to increase representation throughout the educational system.

Establishing Collaborative Relationships: Schools can forge partnerships with local community organizations, such as nonprofit educational foundations, cultural associations, or advocacy groups. These organizations often have established networks and resources to support aspiring educators and can assist in identifying and recruiting diverse teaching candidates.

Mentorship Programs: Collaborating with community organizations that offer mentorship programs, such as Teachers Lounge, Profound Gentlemen and Profound Women can enhance the support available to aspiring teachers. These programs can provide additional mentoring opportunities, networking events, and access to a community of educators who understand the unique challenges and experiences faced by individuals from underrepresented backgrounds.

Resource Sharing and Support: Community organizations can serve as a valuable source of resources, both financial and non-financial, to support aspiring teachers. This can include scholarships, grants, access to educational materials, professional development workshops, and networking opportunities. By leveraging these resources, schools can create a supportive ecosystem that nurtures and uplifts future educators.

Developing a diverse teaching force requires a comprehensive and multifaceted approach. By starting young, creating a talent pipeline, and nurturing potential educators within the community, schools can take proactive steps towards addressing the underrepresentation of black teachers and fostering a more inclusive and equitable educational environment.

Moreover, through partnerships with community organizations, schools can access additional resources and support networks that contribute to the overall success and growth of aspiring educators. By embracing innovative strategies and committing to diversity, equity, and inclusion, we can pave the way for a brighter future in education, where all students have access to exceptional teachers who reflect the rich diversity of our society.

Understanding The Feeder System in Professional Sports

In the world of professional sports, top franchises have recognized the value of developing talent internally through their feeder systems, also known as farm systems. These systems provide a hierarchical structure of teams affiliated with the franchise, allowing young, inexperienced players to develop their skills and progress through the ranks. This chapter explores the lessons that can be learned from professional sports franchises and applied to the education system to enhance student inquiry and education.

The New York Yankees (MLB):

The New York Yankees are renowned for their successful farm system, which has produced numerous star players. The likes of Derek Jeter, Mariano Rivera, and Bernie Williams all honed their skills in the Yankees' minor league system. The franchise's commitment to scouting, player development, and coaching has allowed them to maintain a consistent stream of talented individuals who contribute to their long-term success.

Lesson for Education:

Just as the Yankees have invested in scouting and player development, schools can prioritize identifying potential teachers and supporting them in pursuing a career in education. By providing mentorship, training, and financial assistance, schools can create pathways for aspiring educators and nurture their growth within the system.

The Los Angeles Lakers (NBA):

The Los Angeles Lakers have a strong tradition of developing talent through their G League affiliate, the South Bay Lakers. Players like Alex Caruso and Talen Horton-Tucker have risen through the G League system to become key contributors to the Lakers' success. The franchise recognizes the value of providing young players with opportunities to develop their skills and gain experience in a professional environment.

Lesson for Education:

Schools can create teaching pathways for their support staff, such as paraprofessionals and teacher assistants, by offering professional development, tuition assistance, and incentives. This allows those already familiar with the school's culture and values to transition into certified teaching roles, bringing a sense of loyalty and commitment to the institution.

The Green Bay Packers (NFL):

The Green Bay Packers have a strong history of developing players through their practice squad and minor league system. Their commitment to player development has allowed them to identify and cultivate talent that aligns with the team's culture and playing style. The Packers' success in the draft and talent development has been instrumental in building a consistently competitive team.

Lesson for Education:

Similarly, schools can partner with colleges and universities to provide teaching internships and clinical experiences. This collaboration allows aspiring teachers to gain hands-on experience and learn from experienced educators. By aligning with educational institutions, schools can ensure that their teacher development programs are in sync with the latest research and instructional practices.

The Boston Red Sox (MLB):

The Boston Red Sox boast a successful farm system that has produced notable players like Mookie Betts and Xander Bogaerts. Additionally, they have utilized their minor league prospects as trade assets to acquire major league talent, showcasing the value of investing in player development within the franchise.

Lesson for Education:

Schools can also focus on continuous professional development for their teachers. By providing ongoing training opportunities, educators can improve their instructional skills and stay abreast of the latest educational research and practices. This commitment to professional growth ensures that teachers are equipped with the knowledge and tools necessary to support student inquiry and provide quality education.

The Pittsburgh Penguins (NHL):

The Pittsburgh Penguins have established a strong farm system that has produced exceptional players such as Sidney Crosby and Evgeni Malkin. Their AHL affiliate, the Wilkes-Barre/Scranton Penguins, plays a crucial role in developing young talent. The Penguins' investment in scouting, player development, and coaching has helped them consistently find and nurture top-tier players.

Lesson for Education:

Just as the Penguins have created a strong farm system, schools can implement a grow your own model for developing teachers internally. By identifying potential teachers early on, providing teaching pathways for support staff, partnering with educational institutions, and offering ongoing professional development, schools can build a sustainable pipeline of talented educators who are aligned with the school's culture and instructional practices.

Top sports franchises have demonstrated the effectiveness of feeder systems in developing talent internally.

By applying similar principles to the education system, schools can enhance student inquiry and education by developing their own teachers. Through a grow your own model, schools can identify potential educators, create pathways for staff members, collaborate with educational institutions, and prioritize professional development. This approach builds a strong pipeline of teachers who are committed to the school's mission and values, leading to improved teacher retention and student outcomes.

In addition to developing teachers internally through the "grow your own" model, it is crucial to focus on recruiting and developing more Black teachers. The education system has a significant opportunity to address the lack of diversity in the teaching profession by implementing strategies that specifically target the recruitment and development of Black educators. By incorporating these strategies into the "grow your own" model, schools can make important strides towards creating a more equitable and inclusive education system.

Partnering with local colleges and universities to create pipelines for Black students interested in teaching can open doors and provide necessary support for aspiring Black teachers.

Teacher cadet programs can inspire high school students to pursue teaching careers, providing them with early exposure to the profession and the necessary skills to succeed. Teacher residency programs offer intensive training and mentorship, allowing aspiring Black teachers to gain practical experience and earn their teaching credentials simultaneously.

Professional development opportunities should be tailored to address the unique needs and experiences of Black educators. Mentorship, coaching, and networking opportunities can foster their growth and development, ensuring they have the skills and knowledge needed to excel in the classroom and as leaders within the education system.

Creating a positive school culture that values and supports Black educators is essential. This includes offering competitive salaries that reflect their worth, providing opportunities for professional growth, and fostering an inclusive and equitable environment where their voices are heard and respected.

By implementing these strategies, schools can proactively address the underrepresentation of Black teachers, enhance student experiences, and create a more diverse and inclusive education system. The "grow your own" model, coupled with a focus on recruiting and developing more Black teachers, will contribute to educational equity and help prepare students for a diverse and interconnected world.

Chapter Reflection Questions:

What are the benefits of implementing a "grow your own" model for developing teachers within the school system?

_____

_____

_____

_____

_____

_____

How can the principles and strategies used in professional sports' feeder systems be applied to teacher development within the education system?

_____

_____

_____

_____

_____

_____

In what ways can schools identify and nurture potential teachers within their own communities?

_____

_____

_____

_____

_____

_____

What are the challenges and opportunities associated with developing a diverse and inclusive teaching workforce through a "grow your own" model?

_____

_____

_____

_____

_____

How can the recruitment and development of Black teachers be prioritized within the "grow your own" model?

_____

_____

_____

_____

_____

Chapter Activity:

Imagine you are a school administrator tasked with implementing a "grow your own" model to develop teachers within your school system. Design a comprehensive plan outlining the strategies and steps you would take to recruit, develop, and retain talented educators. Consider the specific needs and goals of your school community, including efforts to increase the representation of Black teachers. Reflect on how this plan aligns with the principles discussed in this chapter and the potential impact it can have on student inquiry and education. Share your plan with a colleague or mentor for feedback and suggestions for improvement.

Chapter Reflection

Use the pages below to write your feelings or reflections from the chapter or take this time to write out your action plan to begin Finding Strategies for Combating the Teacher Shortage and Diversifying the Teacher Workforce

_____

_____

_____

_____

_____

_____

_____

_____

_____

_____

_____

_____

_____

_____

_____

_____

_____

Chapter Six

Build a Championship Culture

"School culture is the heartbeat of an institution, setting the tone for learning, collaboration, and growth." - Unknown

I n the pursuit of educational excellence and equity, it is imperative for schools to not only attract talented educators but also retain them as vital pillars of their teaching community. This chapter delves into the essential task of building a champion culture within the school system, with a specific focus on retaining Black teachers. These educators bring unique perspectives, invaluable experiences, and an unwavering dedication to their students. However, the persistent challenge of retaining Black teachers necessitates a deeper understanding of the reasons behind their departure from the profession. By exploring the top reasons for their attrition and drawing inspiration from the strategies employed by successful sports dynasties, we will uncover actionable steps that school leaders can take to create an inclusive and supportive environment that nurtures and retains Black teachers. Together, we embark on a journey toward fostering a champion culture that embraces diversity, empowers educators, and enriches the lives of all students.

Black educators, like their counterparts from other backgrounds, often face significant hurdles that lead them to leave the teaching profession. In this chapter, we will delve into the top reasons behind their departure and explore the steps we can take to address these challenges. By cultivating a champion culture within the school system, we can create an environment that supports and retains teachers from diverse backgrounds, ensuring an inclusive and equitable learning experience for all students.

One of the primary reasons Black educators leave the profession is the lack of support and resources available to them. Without adequate funding, access to professional development opportunities, or support from district leadership, these teachers can feel overwhelmed and ill-equipped to meet the needs of their students effectively. Jessica, a former Black educator, shares her experience: "I often felt like I was on my own, struggling to provide quality education without the necessary tools and support."

To address this challenge, it is crucial to establish supportive structures within the school system. The first step is to prioritize teacher well-being by providing resources, mentoring programs, and opportunities for professional growth. This can include assigning mentor teachers to guide and support new educators, establishing collaborative networks where teachers can share ideas and best practices, and advocating for increased funding to ensure access to essential teaching resources. These steps will create an environment where Black educators feel valued and supported in their roles.

Inequitable treatment is another critical factor contributing to the departure of Black educators. They may experience disparities such as being assigned lower-performing or more challenging classes, receiving lower salaries compared to their White counterparts, or being denied promotions despite their qualifications. John, a seasoned Black educator, shares his perspective: "It was disheartening to see my White colleagues receive more opportunities and recognition while I felt stagnant in my career."

To promote equity and fairness, school administrators and district leaders must create transparent systems for assigning classes, determining salaries, and making promotions. Regular evaluation and revision of these systems, with a focus on eliminating biases and ensuring equal opportunities for all educators, are essential. Additionally, fostering open dialogue and actively addressing concerns related to inequitable treatment can help build trust and promote a sense of belonging among Black educators.

Burnout and stress are prevalent challenges that affect teachers of all backgrounds, but they can be amplified for Black educators due to systemic racism and cultural differences. These teachers often face the additional burden of combating these challenges while providing quality education to their students. Marcus, a passionate Black educator, emphasizes the need for support: "We need systems in place to address the unique stressors we face, as well as strategies that recognize and celebrate our cultural differences."

To address burnout and stress, it is crucial to prioritize teacher well-being and provide culturally responsive support. This can include implementing practices that acknowledge and validate the experiences of Black educators, offering mental health resources, promoting work-life balance, and providing professional development opportunities that address cultural competency. By incorporating these strategies, we create a nurturing environment that supports the overall well-being of Black educators.

Student behavior and discipline issues can also contribute to the frustration and eventual departure of Black educators. High rates of disciplinary problems and a lack of support in addressing them can create an overwhelming classroom environment. Stephanie, a former Black educator, recounts her struggles: "I often felt helpless and unsupported in dealing with disruptive behavior, and it took a toll on my ability to teach effectively."

To tackle student behavior challenges, it is essential to invest in comprehensive classroom management strategies

and provide teachers with the necessary tools and training. This includes implementing proactive behavior management techniques, establishing clear expectations and consequences, and fostering positive relationships with students.
Additionally, creating a supportive network where teachers
can share strategies and seek guidance can alleviate the feelings
of isolation and provide a platform for collaborative prob-
lem-solving.

Implementing Solutions

Now that we have explored the challenges faced by Black
educators and discussed the steps to address them, let's outline a plan of action to build a champion culture and retain
teachers within the school system:

Establish a Supportive Network: Create mentorship
programs that pair experienced teachers with new educators, facilitating guidance and support. Foster collaboration
through professional learning communities or teacher-led
initiatives, providing opportunities for knowledge sharing
and support.

Review and Revise Policies: Regularly assess and revise
policies to ensure equitable treatment for all educators. Elim-

inate biases in class assignments, salary determinations, and promotion processes, promoting transparency and fairness.

Prioritize Teacher Well-being: Implement strategies to support the well-being of Black educators, such as offering culturally responsive professional development opportunities, providing access to mental health resources, and promoting work-life balance.

Enhance Classroom Management Support: Invest in comprehensive classroom management training and resources for teachers. Implement proactive behavior management strategies, establish clear expectations and consequences, and create a platform for teachers to collaborate and share effective techniques.

By implementing these steps, we can create an environment that addresses the specific challenges faced by Black educators and supports their professional growth and success. Building a champion culture within the school system not only retains talented teachers but also fosters an inclusive and equitable learning environment for all students. As we work together to overcome these challenges, we pave the way for a brighter future in education.

Retention Challenges For Black Teachers in Schools

Retaining black teachers within the education system is a pressing concern, particularly when data reveals that black teachers leave the profession at a significantly higher rate compared to their white counterparts. According to a report by the Learning Policy Institute, the attrition rate for black teachers is 33% higher than that of white teachers. This disparity can be attributed to various reasons.

Firstly, black teachers often encounter a lack of support from school administrators and colleagues, leading to feelings of isolation and a diminished sense of belonging. The absence of a supportive network can contribute to burnout and ultimately drive black teachers to consider leaving the profession. Additionally, black teachers may perceive limited opportunities for advancement within the teaching profession. They may feel that they are not given equal access to professional development programs or leadership roles, impeding their career growth and professional satisfaction.

Racial bias also plays a significant role, as black teachers may face prejudice from students, parents, and colleagues, creating a hostile work environment. These experiences of bias, discrimination, or microaggressions can lead to frustration, emotional exhaustion, and a sense of isolation. Furthermore, pay inequity is a significant concern for black teachers, as they often earn less than their white colleagues with similar levels of education and experience. This disparity in compensation not only affects their financial well-being but also contributes to feelings of undervaluation and frustration.

The high turnover rate among black teachers poses significant challenges for schools and students alike, resulting in a loss of valuable talent and experience. To address this issue, schools must take proactive measures to create a supportive and inclusive environment for black teachers. This can be achieved by fostering a culture of support through mentoring programs, ensuring equal access to professional development opportunities, addressing racial bias through diversity and inclusion training, and promoting pay equity through regular salary audits.

By implementing these steps, schools can create a more supportive and inclusive environment, retaining black teachers as valuable contributors to the teaching profession. The retention of black teachers not only enhances the diversity of perspectives within schools but also enriches the educational experience for all students.

Building a Championship Culture to Retain Black Educators

In order to retain more black educators within the education system, school leaders can learn valuable strategies from successful head coaches such as Joe Torre, Bill Belichick, and Phil Jackson who have built championship cultures. These strategies revolve around creating a strong sense of shared purpose and focusing on the team's goals. By applying these principles, school leaders can create an environment that fosters the retention of black educators.

First and foremost, strong leadership is crucial. School leaders must demonstrate effective leadership by setting clear expectations for their staff and holding everyone accountable. Leading by example, they should promote equity and inclusion, cultivating a culture of respect and collaboration within the school community.

Emphasizing a team-first mentality is another key aspect. School leaders need to highlight the importance of teamwork and foster a sense of community among the staff. This can be accomplished through team-building activities, shared professional development opportunities, and encouraging collaboration on projects. By fostering a cohesive team, school leaders create an environment where black educators feel supported and valued.

Paying attention to the specific challenges faced by black educators is essential. School leaders should actively address these challenges by providing tailored professional development opportunities, creating leadership roles for black educators, and offering support for those experiencing burnout or other difficulties. By acknowledging and proactively addressing these challenges, school leaders create an inclusive environment that promotes the success and well-being of black educators.

Adaptability is also crucial. School leaders should be open to change and willing to adjust their approaches when necessary. Seeking feedback from their staff and being receptive to new strategies ensures that they can effectively address the evolving needs of black educators. This flexibility creates an environment that promotes growth and addresses their concerns.

Building strong relationships with staff, particularly black educators, is paramount. School leaders should invest time in getting to know their staff personally and understanding their unique needs and concerns. Being approachable and open to difficult conversations, while actively seeking feedback, fosters trust and a sense of belonging. This ensures that black educators feel valued and supported.

Consistency is the final element in building a championship culture. School leaders must be reliable, trustworthy, and consistently follow through on their commitments. This consistent approach builds confidence and trust among the staff, creating an environment where everyone feels secure and supported.

By implementing these strategies, school leaders can build a championship culture that attracts and retains more black educators. Creating a sense of shared purpose and emphasizing the team's goals, school leaders can cultivate a supportive and inclusive environment where black educators feel valued and supported. This, in turn, fosters a more diverse and equitable school community, benefiting all students and promoting educational excellence.

Dynasties in sports are not built overnight; they require great leadership and the development of a championship culture that focuses on both talent development and player retention. We can look to iconic franchises like the New York

Yankees from 1996-2000, the New England Patriots in the 2000s, and the Chicago Bulls and LA Lakers for inspiration.

During Joe Torre's tenure as the manager of the New York Yankees, he led the team to four World Series championships in just five years. Torre's success was attributed to his ability to foster a culture of teamwork and resilience. He kept his players focused and motivated, even in the face of challenges. A memorable example was in the 1996 World Series against the Atlanta Braves, where the Yankees lost the first two games. Torre delivered a powerful speech, emphasizing the importance of taking it one game at a time and focusing on winning the next game. The Yankees rallied and went on to win the next four games, securing the championship. Torre's leadership demonstrated his capacity to inspire and motivate his team, enabling them to overcome adversity and achieve greatness.

Likewise, Bill Belichick guided the New England Patriots to an impressive six Super Bowl championships between 2001 and 2018. Belichick created a culture of hard work, meticulous preparation, and attention to detail. He was renowned for his adaptability, adjusting game plans to exploit opponents' weaknesses and making strategic decisions that led to victory.

Phil Jackson, as head coach of the Chicago Bulls and LA Lakers, attained an astounding 11 NBA championships. Jackson cultivated a culture centered around teamwork, selflessness, and mental fortitude. He was known for his remarkable ability to manage high-profile personalities and extract the best from his players. A notable instance showcasing Jackson's coaching prowess occurred during the 1997 NBA Finals against the Utah Jazz. Michael Jordan, the Bulls' star player, was battling the flu and visibly struggling on the court. Jackson made a pivotal decision to rest Jordan for most of the game, entrusting other players to step up and make critical contributions. The Bulls ultimately triumphed, and that game became known as the legendary "Flu Game." Jackson's leadership showcased his capacity to make difficult choices and instill trust in his team during crucial moments.

Drawing inspiration from these championship cultures, school leaders can apply similar strategies to retain more black educators. By fostering teamwork, resilience, hard work, adaptability, and trust, school leaders can build an inclusive and supportive environment that values and retains black educators. Creating a championship culture in schools requires strong leadership, a focus on talent development, and a commitment to retaining valuable educators who contribute to the overall success of the educational community.

Retention Strategies to Cultivate a Champion Culture

Building a champion culture and retaining Black educators within the school system requires a thoughtful approach that goes beyond recruitment. Once educators are brought on board, it becomes crucial to implement effective retention strategies. These strategies aim to create an environment where Black educators feel supported, valued, and motivated to continue their careers within the district. By prioritizing their growth and development, school leaders can cultivate a sense of belonging and foster a culture of success. Here are some key strategies to consider:

First and foremost, provide mentors for new Black educators. Assigning a mentor helps them navigate the district's intricacies, understand its culture, and receive guidance as they settle into their roles. This support system allows them to feel more confident and comfortable in their new environment, ultimately increasing job satisfaction.

Offer ongoing professional development opportunities that are specifically tailored to the needs of Black educators. By investing in their growth, districts demonstrate a commitment to their professional advancement and show appreciation for their unique skills and talents. This continuous learning approach helps educators stay engaged, enhances their effectiveness in the classroom, and opens doors for future career opportunities.

Creating a positive work environment is essential for retaining Black educators. Foster a culture of inclusivity, collaboration, and recognition. Encourage teamwork and celebrate the accomplishments of all educators, including Black educators. Promote diversity and inclusion within the district by valuing and appreciating the unique perspectives and experiences that Black educators bring to the table.

Compensation is a significant factor in retention. Ensure that Black educators are fairly compensated with competitive salaries and comprehensive benefits packages. This recognition of their expertise and experience not only demonstrates their value to the district but also reduces the likelihood of turnover. Compensation should reflect the district's commitment to equity and fairness.

Provide Black educators with opportunities for leadership within the district. This can include serving on committees, leading professional development sessions, or participating in decision-making processes. Empowering them with leadership responsibilities demonstrates trust, respect, and a belief in their potential for growth. These opportunities contribute to their professional development and further engage them in the district's mission.

Establish open lines of communication between Black educators and district leadership. Encourage feedback and create a supportive environment where concerns can be addressed promptly and effectively. By actively listening and responding to their needs, districts build trust and foster a sense of collaboration and partnership.

Recognize and respect cultural differences among Black educators and their students. Provide resources, training, and support that enhance cultural awareness and competency among all educators. Understanding and appreciating diverse backgrounds contribute to a more inclusive and equitable learning environment for all students.

In summary, retaining Black educators requires a comprehensive approach that prioritizes mentorship, professional development, a positive work environment, competitive compensation, leadership opportunities, open communication, and cultural recognition. By implementing these retention strategies, school districts can create a champion culture where Black educators feel valued, supported, and invested in the district's vision of educational excellence.

Retention Strategy #1: Create Incentives to Retain Black Teachers and Educators

Retaining Black teachers and educators is crucial for improving educational outcomes for Black students and cultivating a more diverse and inclusive teaching profession. To achieve this, schools can implement various incentives to encourage the retention of Black teachers and educators.

One effective incentive is offering competitive salaries. When teachers feel valued and fairly compensated for their work, they are more likely to stay in the profession and contribute their expertise to the school community. Additionally, providing professional development opportunities plays a vital role in supporting the growth and success of Black teachers and educators. Mentorship programs, coaching initiatives, and leadership training can enhance their skills and knowledge, while also fostering a supportive environment.

Opportunities for career advancement are another important incentive. Schools can create pathways for growth, such as leadership roles or specialized positions, allowing teachers to pursue their interests while remaining in the classroom. This not only retains valuable talent but also provides job satisfaction and a sense of purpose.

Creating a supportive school culture is essential for retaining Black teachers and educators. By fostering an inclusive environment that values diversity, schools can build relationships, celebrate individual differences, and address bias and discrimination. This inclusive atmosphere promotes a sense of belonging, encouraging teachers to stay in the profession.

Recognizing the importance of work-life balance is another way to retain Black teachers and educators. Offering flexible schedules or part-time work options can accommodate their needs, particularly when they are balancing caregiving responsibilities or pursuing other interests outside the classroom.

Lastly, schools can explore student loan forgiveness programs as an incentive. By reducing the financial burden of student loans, these programs make the teaching profession more appealing and accessible to aspiring Black teachers. As you develop an incentive based program to increase retention, organizations such as Teach Like Me and Housing For Teachers are amazing organizations that aim to increase the number of black teachers by removing the existing barriers to entry and provide support needed for all students.

By implementing these incentives, schools can demonstrate their commitment to retaining Black teachers and educators, fostering a diverse and inclusive teaching profession, and ultimately improving educational outcomes for Black students.

Building a champion culture and retaining Black teachers within the school system requires a multifaceted approach. By addressing the key factors that contribute to the departure of Black educators, such as lack of support, inequitable treatment, burnout, student behavior, lack of diversity, limited advancement opportunities, and low pay, schools can create a more inclusive and equitable learning environment. School leaders can draw inspiration from successful sports dynasties that exemplified strong leadership, a team-first mentality, attention to detail, adaptability, strong relationships, and consistency.

By implementing these strategies, coupled with specific retention strategies like mentorship, professional development, career advancement opportunities, supportive school culture, work-life balance, and incentives, schools can retain more Black teachers and educators, nurturing a diverse and talented teaching workforce that positively impacts the educational experiences and outcomes of Black students. Ultimately, by cultivating a champion culture, schools can build a stronger foundation for academic excellence, equity, and social progress within their communities.

Chapter Reflection Questions:

What are the top reasons behind the attrition of Black teachers in the education profession?

_____

_____

_____

_____

_____

_____

How can school leaders prioritize teacher well-being and provide the necessary support and resources to retain Black educators?

_____

_____

_____

_____

_____

_____

What strategies can be implemented to address inequitable treatment and promote fairness among Black educators?

_____

_____

_____

_____

_____

_____

How can burnout and stress be addressed for Black educators, taking into account the unique challenges they face?

_____

_____

_____

_____

_____

_____

What steps can schools take to tackle student behavior and discipline issues that contribute to the frustration of Black educators?

_____

_____

_____

_____

_____

Chapter Activity:

Imagine you are a school leader responsible for creating a champion culture that retains Black teachers. Develop an action plan outlining specific steps you would take to address the challenges identified in the chapter and create an inclusive and supportive environment for Black educators. Consider strategies for mentorship, professional development, equity and fairness, well-being support, and classroom management. Share your action plan and discuss it with colleagues or mentors to gather feedback and refine your approach.

Chapter Reflection

Use the pages below to write your feelings or reflections from the chapter or take this time to write out your action plan to begin Finding Strategies for Combating the Teacher Shortage and Diversifying the Teacher Workforce

_____

_____

_____

_____

_____

_____

_____

_____

_____

_____

_____

_____

_____

_____

_____

_____

Diversifying The Teacher Workforce

"Diversity is not about how we differ. Diversity is about embracing one another's uniqueness." - Ola Joseph

Throughout the book, we have embarked on a transformative journey to combat the teacher shortage and diversify the teacher workforce. As we conclude this chapter on diversifying the teacher workforce, it is essential to recap the key themes and strategies discussed throughout the book. We have explored the past and present state of education, envisioned the future of the educational industry, and delved into the most valuable processes that schools and teachers can implement to enhance the school experience.

In our exploration of the past, we have confronted the historical underrepresentation of certain communities within the teaching profession. We have examined the systemic barriers and biases that have perpetuated a lack of diversity and hindered the potential of our education system. Acknowledging this reality is the first step towards creating meaningful change and building a more inclusive educational environment.

Looking towards the future, we envision an educational industry that reflects the rich tapestry of our society. We aspire to a future where students of all backgrounds can see themselves represented in their teachers, role models, and mentors. By fostering diversity in the teaching workforce, we pave the way for enhanced cultural understanding, increased student engagement, and improved academic outcomes.

Throughout this book, we have emphasized the importance of identifying and recruiting exceptional prospects to teach in the classroom. We have explored strategies for reaching out to diverse communities, dispelling stereotypes, and showcasing the rewards and impact of a career in education. By actively seeking out talented individuals from various backgrounds, we can tap into a wealth of perspectives, experiences, and talents that will enrich the learning environment.

However, recruitment alone is not enough. Retention and development play vital roles in building a championship culture within our schools. We have explored the significance of mentorship, professional development opportunities, and creating a supportive work environment where educators of all backgrounds feel included, valued, and supported. By investing in the growth and well-being of our teachers, we create a foundation for success that extends to our students.

In our pursuit of a diverse and inclusive teaching profession, we recognize that this journey requires continuous effort and commitment. We must challenge biases, address systemic inequities, and foster a culture of belonging within our educational institutions. By recognizing and valuing the unique contributions of every educator, regardless of their race, ethnicity, gender, or background, we create an environment that celebrates diversity, encourages collaboration, and prepares our students to thrive in a diverse world.

"The MVPs of Education" has aimed to serve as a catalyst for change in the educational system. We have highlighted the importance of diversity and inclusion as central to the success of our students and the advancement of our society. Our goal is to empower educators, administrators, and policymakers with the tools, strategies, and insights necessary to transform the educational landscape.

As we conclude this book, let us remember our purpose: to enhance the educational system through diversity and inclusion, empowering our students to reach their fullest potential. Each one of us has the power to make a difference in the lives of students, and by working together, we can build an educational system that embraces the strength of diversity, fosters a culture of inclusivity, and ensures a brighter future for generations to come.

By embracing diversity and inclusion, we pave the way for a more equitable and enriched educational experience for all. Let us continue to champion diversity in the teaching workforce, nurture the growth of our educators, and create an educational environment where every student feels valued, supported, and empowered to achieve greatness. Together, we can create an educational system that truly reflects the vibrant mosaic of our society and prepares our students to thrive in an ever-changing world.

About The Author

Blake Nathan is a trailblazing education reformer who is on a mission to transform the education system as we know it. As an Atlanta native, he graduated from The Tennessee State University with a bachelor's degree in Aeronautical and Industrial Technology, majoring in Aviation Flight. He went on to become a Woodrow Wilson National Teaching Fellow and obtained a master's degree in technology from Purdue University.

After working as a classroom teacher in Indianapolis, Blake recognized the need for change within the education sector. He founded the Educate ME Foundation with the aim of diversifying the teaching population and creating a culture where the presence of African American males and females, as well as teachers of color, is normalized.

Under Blake's leadership, the Educate ME Foundation has garnered national attention for its innovative approach to tackling the teacher shortage and creating a more diverse teaching workforce. Blake is also a devoted husband, father, and man of faith, and he is committed to using his platform to create a brighter future for students and educators alike. His new book, The MVPs of Education: Strategies for Combating the Teacher Shortage and Diversifying the Teacher Workforce, offers practical insights and solutions for addressing some of the most pressing challenges facing the education system today.

www.ingramcontent.com/pod-product-compliance
Lightning Source LLC
Chambersburg PA
CBHW041041050426
42335CB00056B/3242